The Breast Milk of the Volcano

Bolivia and the Atacama Desert

For *The Breast Milk of the Volcano*, Unknown Fields travel through the energy-rich landscapes of the Bolivian Salt Lakes and the Atacama Desert to see where the city stores its electricity. Here the ground is charged with potential, for buried beneath the mirror of the world's largest salt flat, the Salar De Uyuni, is a grey gold called lithium, the key ingredient in batteries, a substance in every one of our pockets, in every gleaming device, and every electric car. As Elon Musk announces his latest vehicle, his residential power unit, his solar revolution, the drive for small and powerful batteries has rendered this landscape one of the most sought after on earth. We chase the grey rush to the ancient salt flats, a landscape of Incan mythology and sacred mountains. A traditional indigenous narrative describes this shimmering white expanse being created from the mixing of the tears and breast milk of a jilted mother volcano. Over half of the world's reserves of lithium lie under these ethereal inverted skies. This is the feeding ground of the new green energy revolution, pregnant with billion dollar prospects. Still largely undeveloped it is a territory of possibility, on the verge of change, a proving ground in a state of becoming. If the future
is electric then the future is here, lying in wait for the world.

    Unknown Fields chronicle this electric landscape, investigating the infrastructures that serve as energy conduits — translating matter like a luminous language, from a hole in the ground to the glow of our phones — to trace a wild journey of electrons from the radiant gizmos of our technologies deep into landscapes far, far away. This book is an account of a contemporary creation story for our energy, from the Big Bang to the battery, from the birth of lithium at the beginning of the universe to the low power warning flashing on our screens. We power our future with the breast milk of volcanoes.

23°
01'
24.8"
S
67°
45'
13.3"
W

In the beginning, the beginning of the beginning, seconds from zero, 13.8 billion years ago, the creation story of lithium begins. Big. Bang.

It was there, at the dawn of time, alongside helium and hydrogen, one of only three elements able to claim their ultimate origin in that hot dense primordial gas. From this interstellar matter hydrogen and helium sparked the light of the first stars and as they cooled below two trillion degrees lithium was formed. The glow of the birth of the cosmos, forged in the fallout fragments of cosmic ray collisions, had started its journey. Light is the only detectable record that is left of the Big Bang, it is the ghost of lithium creation.

At five kilometres above sea level on the Chajnantor Plateau in the Chilean Atacama desert, the landscape has eyes. Sixty-six white pupils turn in unison to search the thin air of these dark skies. In the extinct indigenous language Kunza, Chajnantor translates as 'taking off place' and here the astrophysicists at Atacama's Large Millimeter Array observatory are focused skyward, travelling deep through the dark interstellar clouds of the coldest, oldest parts of the universe. They gaze beyond the slice of the visible spectrum, between far infrared and radio waves, feeding terabyte upon terabyte of information into a supercomputer with the power of three million laptops. The array of super natural eyes drift across the volcanic crater, dragged by two 28-wheeler beasts, Otto and Lore, the observatory's antennae transporters. Powered by four formula one engines and herded by Alfredo, the only person on earth qualified to drive them, they rearrange the dishes to focus their field of view, to act as a single giant lens, the largest in all of history.

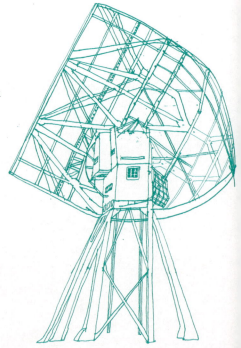

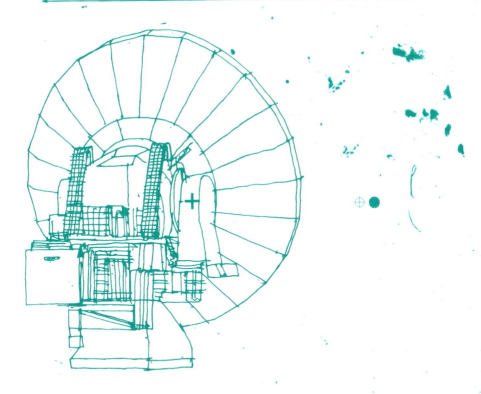

Another community of nomadic shepherds, the indigenous Likanantay people, used to own this land and trekked across the grounds where the antennae now stand. On the Chajnantor plateau all eyes have always been on shadows in the sky. Silhouetted against the light of the Milky Way the dark clouds that ALMA observe are the same shadow constellations of indigenous mythology, the animals that came to drink at that celestial river Mayu and the dark nebula of the great rift. Dancing within a swathe of the interstellar cloud that forged lithium is Yacana the llama, her baby and her shepherd, the serpent Mach'acuay and Atoq the fox who pursues Hanp'atu the toad and Yutu-Tinamou the bird across the sky. These creatures have carried lithium, the lightest of metals from the beginning of time, to the crust of the earth.

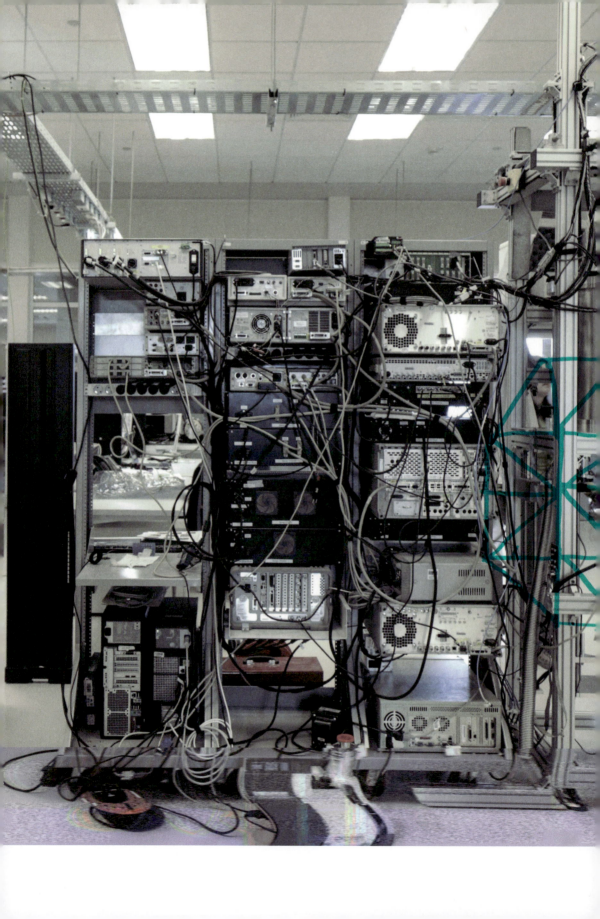

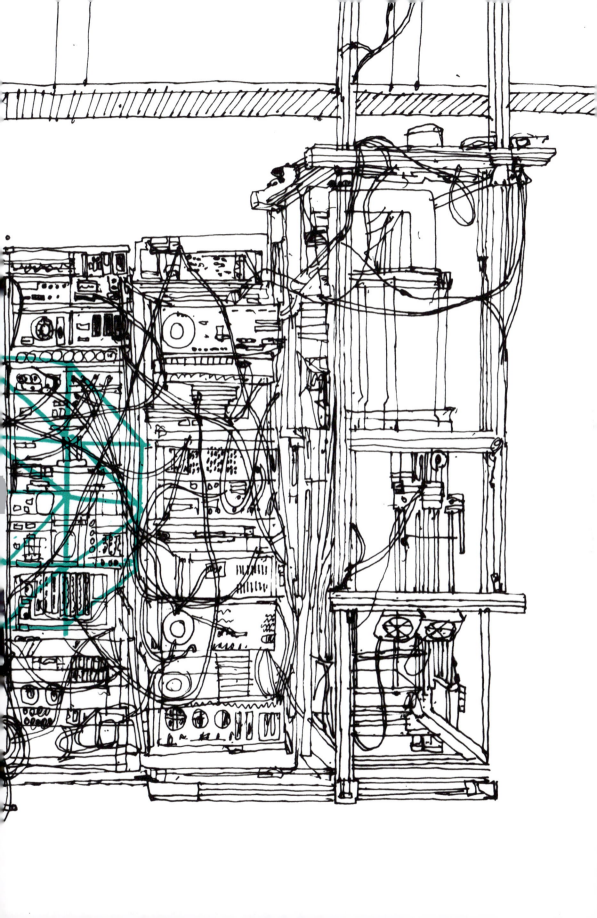

4.6

20°
07'
43.1"
S
67°
31'
16.3"
W

4.6 BILLION YEARS

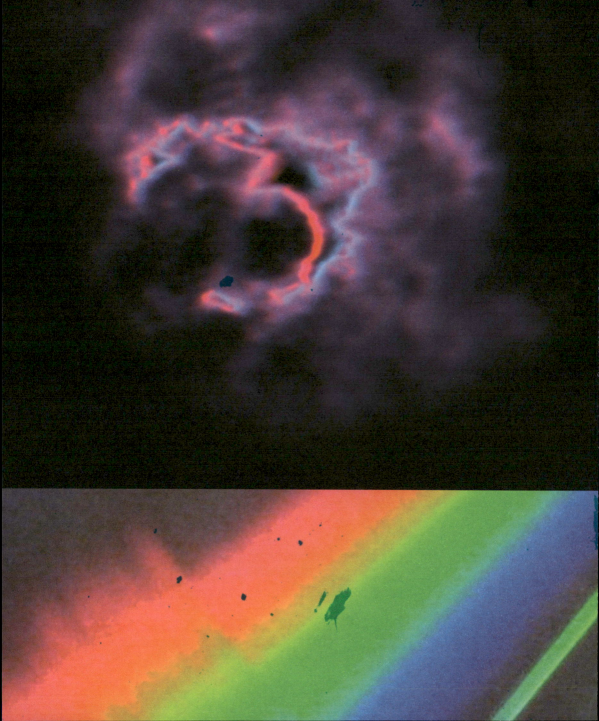

4.6 billion years ago, as Yacana drank from the sky, the wreckage of an exploding supernova slowly began to condense into our planet. In this vast cloud of swirling cosmic matter, gravity and violent collapse gave shape to the sphere of the earth and embedded within it the traces of lithium. As paths of a new solar system loop and stretch three electrons orbit a nucleus. Li – atomic number 3. A silvery metal, shimmering, soft enough to be cut with a knife, just light enough to float in water. It gives a crimson note to a flame and burns with a white hot dazzle. It is magical, mysterious and volatile. From the Greek 'lithos', meaning stone, it is the lightest of all metals. It pops and fizzes and cannot freely occur in nature as it reacts so violently with air and water. Instead, it takes its form in small units, in nearly all igneous rocks and many mineral springs. Lithium comprises seven parts per million of the planet's crust. Locked in the ground, waiting for release, an electric earth.

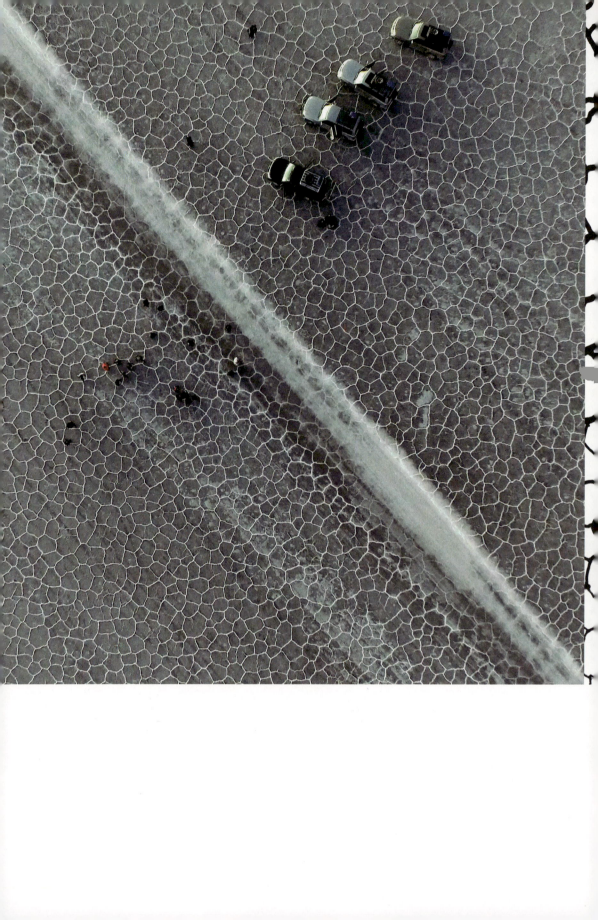

Ten thousand years ago a series of lakes formed high on the Andean plateau, where Chile, Bolivia and Argentina, the three countries of the lithium triangle, now meet. Here lies the largest salt lake on the planet, stretching across ten thousand square kilometres of Bolivia, formed from ten billion tons of salt and containing at least 50% of the world's lithium reserves. Resources have always been extracted by the indigenous cultures of the region but precious metals and stones were traditionally thought to be alive. Here gold is not mined, it is grown, and mountains give birth to minerals.

    The salt lake was once a vast plain where the Incan giants lived. Among them was the beautiful Tunupa who was courted by all the men of the tribe. She chose to marry Cuzco, a strong young man, and a son called Calicatin was soon born of their union. Cuzco would only leave her to trade salt, bartering for food and resources across the valleys. While away on one of his journeys he became infatuated with a pretty young woman called Cruzuña and they ran off together, never to return. Driven by curiosity Calicatin went in search of his father and Tunupa chased after him. All day and all night she searched and tried in vain to bring her child back. The gods, tired of the giant's lies, secrecy and betrayal, decided to punish them all and petrified them as mountains. Tunupa began to cry, a volcano spewing ash and rock from the depths of the planet, rich in light elements like magnesium, potassium, boron and lithium. While the tears rolled down her cheeks, her breasts began to lose the milk that her son had not suckled. Millennia of meltwater from the snowcapped peaks of her mountain seeped down through her rocky sides, leaching minerals into the lake below. As the giants became volcanoes, Tunupa's tears ran into subterranean brine and her milk crystallised as the crusty salt skin that now stretches across the plateau. As the sun sets, her mountain shadow is now cast across its crisp, blinding surface and disappears into night.

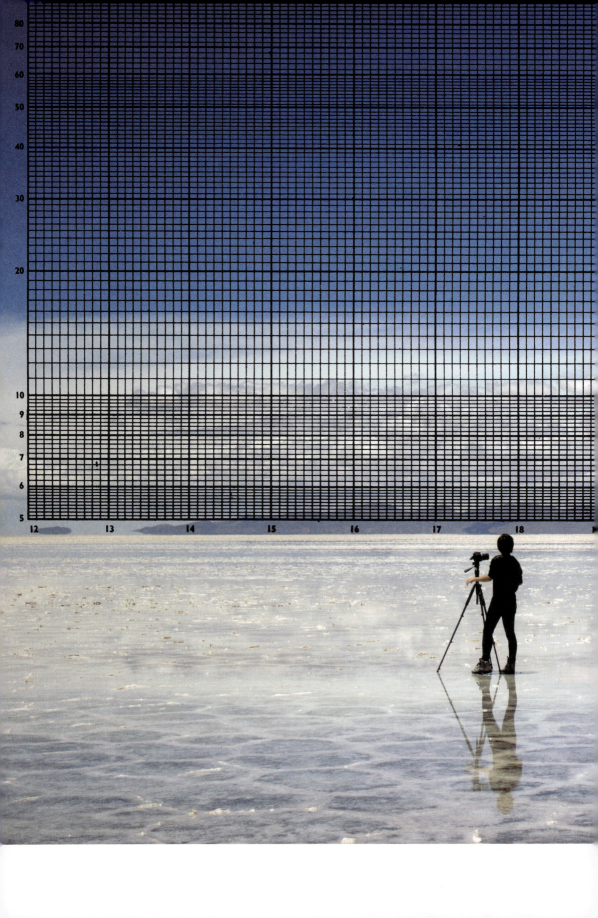

Before the Spanish language arrived indigenous groups referred to the salt lake as Lake Tunupa but now it is known as the Salar de Uyuni. In the depths of its reflections, the Salar hides a resource on the verge of becoming one of the most sought after on earth. The flattest, whitest place in existence, so large and consistent that it is focused on by orbiting satellites, who use it to calibrate their altimeters. This charged landscape, this electric earth, remote and unforgiving, is now quantified for its energy potential. These are new beginnings, new resource fields, new dynamics of demand and dependency. This natural wonder has become a lucrative investment and has cast Bolivia as the Saudi Arabia of the electric age.

Today Tunupa and Calicatin are frozen on opposite sides of the Salar. Between them the largest salt pan on the planet, the biggest battery we could ever need, the core of our technology and the future of green energy.

20°
32'
29.3"
S
67°
22'
19.4"
W

Ref FT 5

'RESEARCH' EXTENSOMETER
Sample No.
Date Tested
Water Absorption
Sample Data: —

14S0-20

48   49   50   51   52   53   54   55
              *

It was a little over 20 years ago that lithium erupted again in the Salar de Uyuni. A Belgian construction company was turning ground to build a road to connect the local communities that now ring the Giant's Basin. They found a ground too soft for construction but inadvertently cracked open the earth to reveal the lithium-rich brine below. A hundred million tons of Tunupu's forgotten tears are now estimated to be trapped here. It has taken all this time but now cities, industries and infrastructures are jostling to feed at the shores of this ancient lake and play out our electric dreams.

    With the salt crunching under his well-worn shoes Franscisco Quisbert, or Comrade Lithium as he is now known, stalks the lake and squints in the reflected light. He is the modern giant of Uyuni. Through salt mining, generations after generations have been nurtured by this breast milk and he is determined to ensure that his people will continue to be so. In the shadows an American-Canadian company called Litco had been busy buying up the exclusive mining rights to the Salar and setting in motion plans to ship all the revenue from extraction out of the country. In response Comrade Lithium founded FRUCTUS, an indigenous activist group that rallied against the multinational, resisting the typical patterns of exploitation that often beset a developing but resource-rich nation. The lithium dreams of Bolivia are now based around the development of a national lithium industry, Bolivian battery manufacture and a powerful energy economy. Made in Bolivia, for Bolivia and exported to the world. Without the knowledge and assistance of foreign companies it has taken over 20 years but now Bolivia is ready and the Salar is soon to be industrialised. The comrade has retired, returned to his farm in the foothills of the volcano and the giants watch on, as their lake is turned inside out.

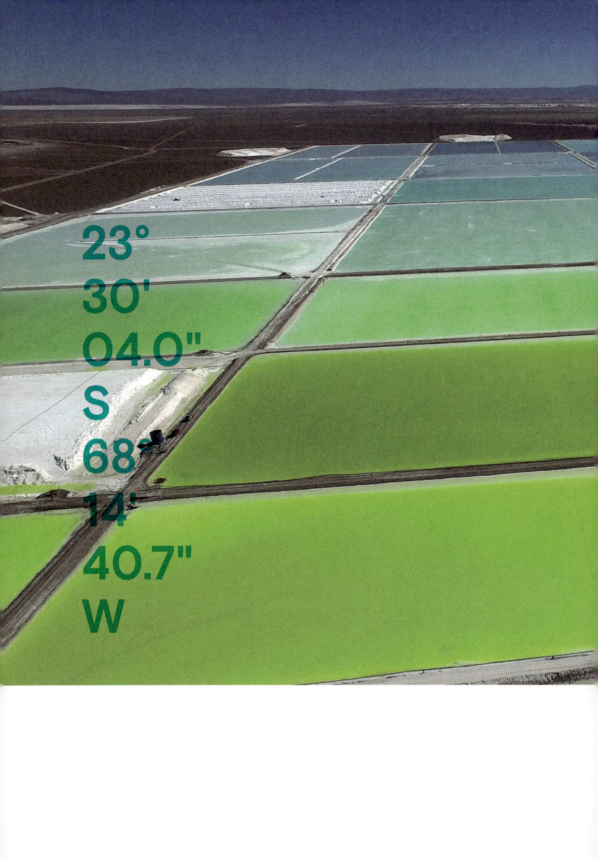

You cannot see it on the desperately flat horizon, or access it by any public road. Its mystery is protected by its isolation. Locals speak of the metal sea but none have seen it and they can only point in its vague direction. Bolivia is a landlocked nation but it once had a coastline before this was taken away by Chile. The country had lost its natural ocean, but now it has created another. If the landscape is the character of Salar mythology then what stories do we tell of an artificial sea?

    The only way to see it is from the air and when you escape the cracked surface and look down, what was once the crystal white expanse of the Salar de Uyuni has been flooded with a surreal painted sea. Since 2008, the sun has been beating down on a new liquid landscape, a territorial alchemy translating the lake pumped up from beneath the salt from blue to green to yellow, from worthless diluted brine to a concentrated pool of one of the most valuable elements on earth. There are no waves in the metal sea, no currents, just stillness. This is an ocean without life. Lithium development is mining through evaporation rather than extraction. A tessellated ocean of evaporative ponds where each shift in hue signals a rising concentration of lithium salts. The shores of the metal sea begin at Pond no 15, 0.2% lithium, the least concentrated, azure blue with a sodium chloride beach. Each month the ponds are drained and transferred to the next in line, and each month the colour changes and the lithium gets richer. A group of mine workers called Rock Lickers monitor the process, reading the sea and deciding when it's right to move on. Across 15 months the sea migrates through the holding pools of the Salar until it reaches the deep coffee waters of Pond no 1, 6% lithium sulphate. Shimmering pools of azure, turquoise, cyan blues have faded to viridian and khaki greens and on to muddy yellows. This sea that has been slowly evolving over billions of years is now ready to leave the land of giants forever, sucked up by

a convoy of thirsty 18-wheelers and driven off
the Salar to the lithium carbonate refinery.
What is left behind is a massive quantity of
table salt piled up beside the lithium ocean and
gradually a new mother mountain grows. What will
we call her, this crystal volcano? A totem for a
sacrificial sea, evaporating to keep the screens
glowing and the wheels turning.

The trucks roll into the refinery. Here the
liquid is transformed from lithium sulphate
of the tessellated sea to the lithium carbonate
required for battery production. Calcium oxide is
first added to eliminate contaminants and finally
carbonate is introduced. Commercial grade lithium
carbonate that is used in industrial applications
has a purity of 95%, battery grade is 99.5% and
99.99% lithium carbonate is used in medical
applications such as treating mental illness.
What began in the stellar soup of the Big Bang
is now ready for the battery.

There are rooms in the refinery that have never
been photographed before as all these processes
are now being patented. The technology of lithium
is being developed here in Bolivia, by Bolivians,
for Bolivians. It is a country in a stage of
decolonisation, a radical refusal of foreign
involvement. Here being indigenous is not just
a racial or ethnic issue, it is about being
collectively able to own, live in and care for
a place. The creation story of a battery has
become the creation of a nation.

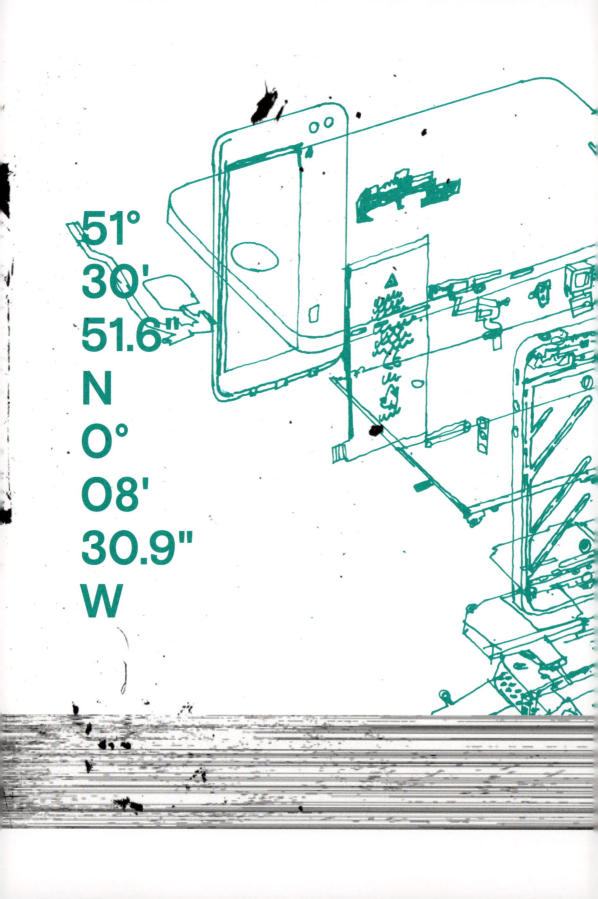

The iPhone 6 can travel 14 hours on its 1810 mAh lithium polymer battery before it comes to rest. It is the last thing we look at before we sleep and millions caress it with a tenderness reserved for no other. It feels warm to the touch and we are told stories by marketing companies about its lightness, and its slim lines. Reflected in its pristine polished glass is the mirrored expanse of the crystal white salt lake from which it has been wrenched. Nearly 9 billion mobile phones in the world are powered by lithium-ion batteries. Billions of the same phones are discarded every year. 5–10 grams of Tunupa's tears and breast milk is contained in each iPhone.

FIG. 4

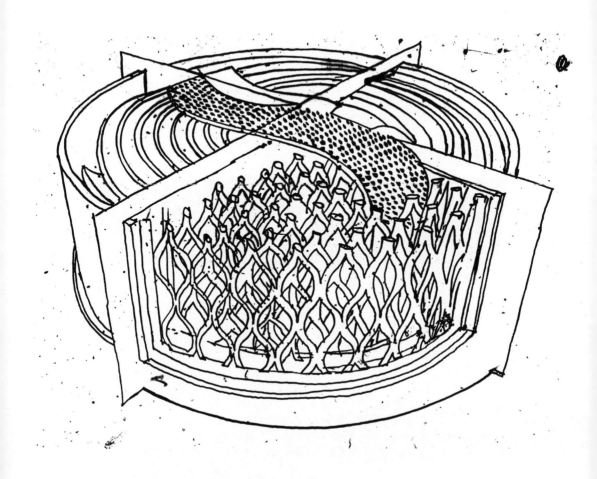

In *ludicrous mode* the 7000 lithium nickel cobalt aluminum oxide (LiNiCoAlO2) cells of the 90kWh battery pack that sits in the belly of the newly born Tesla p90d delivers enough power to accelerate from 0 to 60 miles per hour in 2.8 seconds. 20–30 kilograms of lithium are at the core of each electric car. Demand for lithium is set to outstrip supply by 2023. As this glistening beast shrieks down the tarmac it sends ripples across the turquoise pools of lithium brine. It is a hunter, stalking the electric future.

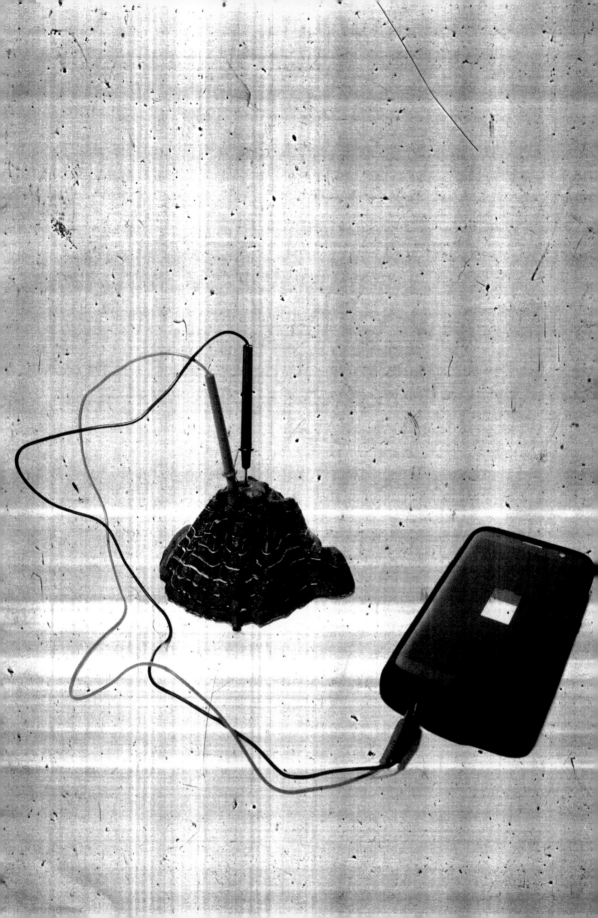

Three electrons orbit the lithium nucleus. Our story began with the travels of stars and ends with these tiny revolving planets waiting for a charge. These little lithium-ion packets of electrochemical reaction were pioneered at Oxford University in the 1970s and turned into a commercial technology by Sony, who produced the first lithium-ion batteries in the early 1990s. Since then, due to their high charge to weight ratio, they have become the linchpin of a post-hydrocarbon future.

    A rechargeable lithium-ion battery is formed from a number of power-generating compartments called cells. Each cell has three elements, a positive electrode or anode, a negative electrode or cathode, and a chemical electrolyte that flows around them. At the core of this entire story is lithium's property as an ideal battery anode material, high in electrochemical potential. When the battery is charging, the positive electrode gives up some of its lithium ions, which travel through the electrolyte to the negative, electrode. The battery accumulates energy during this process. As the battery discharges, the lithium ions drift back across the electrolyte to the positive electrode, creating the energy that powers our technologies. With every charge they get closer to death, they burn bright but might live for two or three years before they turn to stone again. Lithos.

The lonely jilted volcano spills tears and breast milk of lithium brine, and powers a phone. 4%, 3%, 2%, we get to know the behaviour of its percentages, its lithium battery waning as we type, tap, swipe, as we Google the answer to our every waking wondering. 'I'm on 1%' 'my phone is dying' … almost dead. Almost dark.

Unknown Fields have built a glass battery – a mythic love story that trickle charges a phone, bringing it back from the brink with a life-giving juice. While the world does its best to ignore that technology is forged from the earth, with marketing campaigns of ephemeral clouds and the relentless push for the smallest and lightest, this object embodies the story of the landscape in which it was made. A mass of alternating aluminium and graphite – anode and cathode – submerged in a lithium brine electrolyte collected from Bolivia's electric Salar de Uyuni creates a slow reaction, the drip charge of a weeping volcano. The creation myth of this landscape is told again and again as the electrons flow.

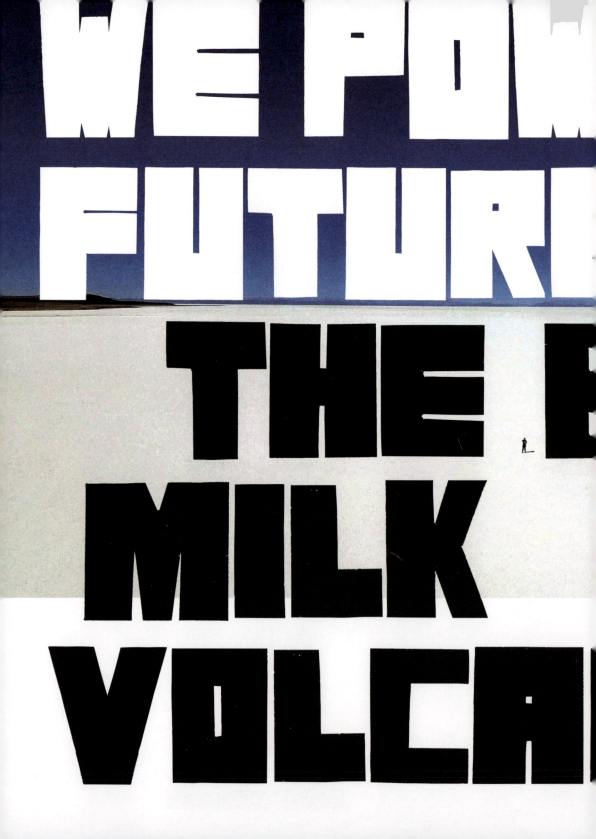

ER OUR
WITH
REAST
OF
OES

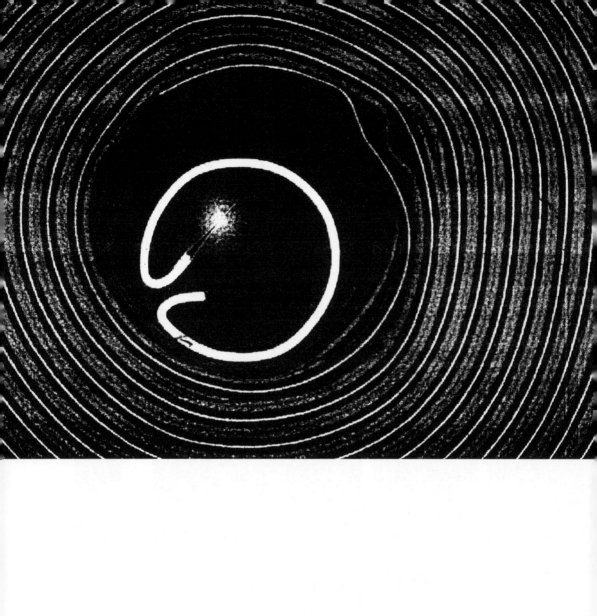

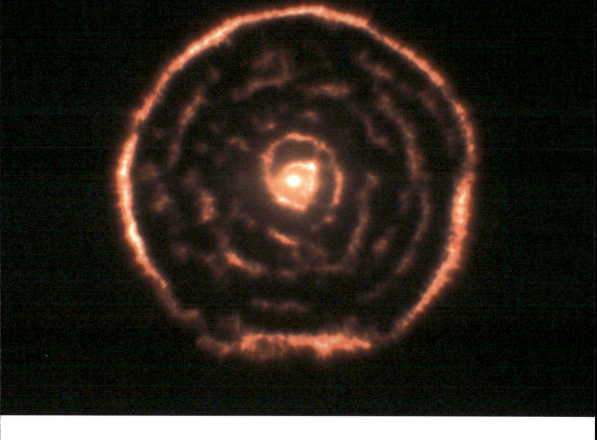

This millisecond dance of ions has set in motion
our dreams of the green electric revolution.
The untold story of this brave new now has been
billions of years in the making, from spiral
galaxies to the spiral wound electrodes of a
battery cell. The flash of the Big Bang to the
flash of an electron. Our future is powered by
the breast milk of volcanoes.

The Breast Milk of the Volcano by Unknown Fields

Design: Neasden Control Centre & City Edition Studio
Illustration: Neasden Control Centre

Printed in Italy by Musumeci S.p.a.
ISBN 978-1-907896-84-2

© 2016 Architectural Association and the Author

No part of this book may be reproduced in any manner whatsoever without written permission from the publisher, except in the context of reviews

For a catalogue of AA Publications visit
aaschool.ac.uk/publications or email publications@aaschool.ac.uk

AA Publications
36 Bedford Square
London
WC1B 3ES
t + 44 (0)20 7887 4021
f + 44 (0)20 7414 0783